To:

From:

Photographs copyright © 2009 AP Images

Designed by Heather Zschock

Copyright © 2009
Peter Pauper Press, Inc.
202 Mamaroneck Avenue
White Plains, NY 10601
All rights reserved
ISBN 978-1-59359-844-0
7 6 5 4 3 2
Visit us at www.peterpauper.com

Women Who Dared

Written and compiled by
Evelyn Beilenson
and Lois Kaufman

Introduction by Barbara Paulding

PETER PAUPER PRESS, INC.
White Plains, New York

Contents

Introduction

Be bold. If you're going to make
an error, make a doozy, and don't
be afraid to hit the ball.

BILLIE JEAN KING

The proving ground on which we stand as women is comprised of milestones achieved by our visionary sisters of past and present. From all walks of life and with a colorful range of accomplishments, these notable women triumphed against the odds in opening doors for those who followed—from Susan B. Anthony, whose tireless efforts helped women attain the right to vote, all the way to Hillary Clinton, who garnered 18 million votes in her bid for the Democratic nomination for president, before becoming secretary of state.

The world is a better place because these women lived and pursued their passions, however humble or even outrageous. What Rachel Carson, author of *Silent Spring*, did for environmentalism, Rosa Parks did for civil rights, Madame Curie did for science, Helen Keller did for the blind, Coco Chanel

did for fashion, and Gloria Steinem did for women's rights. This tribute to daring women honors those who have challenged the status quo, ever expanding the field of possibilities.

Life is either a daring adventure, or nothing at all.

HELEN KELLER

Abigail Adams

Early advocate of women's rights
1744-1818

*Remember the ladies, and be more generous
and favorable to them than your ancestors.*

Although Abigail Adams, a highly intelligent woman, was educated at home, she came to feel that women deserved public education equal to that provided for men. As first lady, she also advocated emancipation of African-American slaves. Her letters, some of which were published posthumously, reveal how much she influenced the presidency of her husband, John Adams.

Corazon Aquino

**Led her country from dictatorship
to democracy**
1933-

*I would rather die a meaningful death
than to live a meaningless life.*

Succeeding her assassinated husband as
president of the Philippines from 1986 to
1992, Corazon Aquino reestablished democratic
institutions and achieved social and
economic reforms, turning over a well-run
nation to her successor. *Time* magazine
named her 1986 Woman of the Year, and
she was awarded the Fulbright Prize for
International Understanding in 1996.

Marian Anderson

**Legendary singer and
civil rights trailblazer**
1897-1993

*I have a great belief in the future
of my people and my country.*

Marian Anderson, a great American contralto, was barred from singing in Constitution Hall by the DAR in 1939 because of her race. First Lady Eleanor Roosevelt resigned from the DAR and arranged for her to sing at the Lincoln Memorial, where she drew a crowd of 75,000. In 1955 she made a precedent-setting debut as the first black woman to sing solo at the Metropolitan Opera.

Susan B. Anthony

Women's rights advocate; first woman to be honored on an American coin
1820–1906

The true republic—men, their rights and nothing more; women, their rights and nothing less.

In 1872 Susan B. Anthony was arrested for challenging the New York election law by casting her vote. A prominent suffragette, Anthony fought for women's rights her entire life, serving as president of the National American Woman Suffrage Association until she was 80. She also worked tirelessly for abolitionism, education, labor reform, and temperance.

Josephine Baker

First African-American woman to become a world-famous entertainer
1906-1975

A violinist had a violin, a painter his palette. All I had was myself. I was the instrument I must care for.

At the age of 19, Josephine Baker left the U.S. for Paris and became one of Europe's best known entertainers for the next 50 years. She worked undercover for the French Resistance during World War II, for which she later received the Croix de Guerre. She refused to perform for segregated audiences in the U. S., and in 1963, she marched on Washington beside Martin Luther King, Jr.

Clara Barton

Founder of the American Red Cross
1821-1912

*I cannot afford the luxury of a closed mind.
I go for anything new that might
improve the past.*

During the Civil War, Clara Barton distributed food and medical supplies to the wounded. After learning about the International Red Cross and the Geneva Convention while in Europe in 1869, she founded the American Red Cross and persuaded the U.S. to accept the standards of the Geneva Convention on the treatment of the war wounded.

Avril "Kim" Campbell

First woman prime minister of Canada

1947-

*Canadians want to see real hope restored,
not false hopes raised.*

Determined and ambitious, Kim Campbell can claim many "firsts" for women: first female minister of justice and attorney general of Canada; first female minister of national defense; first female elected leader of the Progressive Conservative Party of Canada; and, in 1993, elected to be the first female prime minister of Canada.

Margaret Bourke-White

First woman official U.S. war correspondent

1906-1971

Usually I object when someone makes overmuch of men's work versus women's work, for I think it is the excellence of the results which counts.

Noted for being the first U.S. reporter let into Russia after the revolution, Margaret Bourke-White was also well known for her photographs of the Great Depression, World War II, and the liberation of Buchenwald concentration camp. She served *Life* magazine as photojournalist and editor for 33 years.

Rachel Carson

**Founder of the modern
environmental movement**
1907-1964

*Those who dwell among the beauties
and mysteries of the earth are never
alone or weary of life.*

Biologist and writer on science and nature,
Rachel Carson set off a national contro-
versy on the use of pesticides when she
published *Silent Spring* in 1962. A best-
seller, the book boldly challenged the agri-
cultural and chemical industries and the
government, and spawned landmark environmental protections.

Gabrielle "Coco" Chanel

Designer who fundamentally changed women's fashion
1883-1971

Fashion fades; only style remains the same.

French designer Coco Chanel revolutionized women's fashion. She freed women from corseted clothes and introduced a casual and simple look. Coco popularized short hair, shorter skirts, and gave the world the little black dress and her famous No. 5 perfume. Overcoming childhood adversity, she learned to sew in an orphanage, and by 1920 Coco had her own couture house, still a force in fashion today.

Mary Cassatt

First American Impressionist painter
1844-1926

*I have touched with a sense of art
some people—they felt the love and the life.
Can you offer me anything to compare
to that joy for an artist?*

American artist Mary Cassatt moved to
France in 1874, studying with Degas and
exhibiting with Impressionists and alone.
A show of her work at the Philadelphia
Academy of Fine Arts in 1876 introduced
Impressionism to the U.S. Almost blind
and unable to paint in her later years, Cassatt became involved in women's suffrage,
with her characteristic audacity.

Julia Child

Celebrity chef . . . and spy
1912-2004

Life itself is the proper binge.

Julia Child may be known mostly as a television chef, but during World War II, she was a spy for the American Office of Strategic Services (OSS), gathering information to combat the Nazis. In 1946, she married Paul Child, who aroused her interest in French cooking. She then learned the techniques herself, and went on to teach—in her own inimitable style—via her cookbooks and award-winning television programs.

Shirley Chisholm

**First black woman to be
elected to Congress**
1924-2005

*In the end antiblack, antifemale, and all
forms of discrimination are equivalent to
the same thing—antihumanism.*

Born in Brooklyn, New York, Shirley
Chisholm was the first black female elected
to Congress, where she served from 1969
to 1983. She was also the first black
woman to run for president, in 1972.
Chisholm's legacy is as a fierce advocate
and spokesperson for women, minorities,
the poor, and the working class.

Hillary Rodham Clinton

**First lady, senator, and
secretary of state**
1947-

*In too many instances, the march to global-
ization has also meant the marginalization
of women and girls. And that must change.*

After having been first lady from 1992 to
2000, Hillary Clinton moved to New York
State, where she won a seat in the Senate.
She was reelected to a second term in 2006.
Clinton ran for the Democratic nomination for president in 2008, garnering 18
million votes and eventually conceding to
Barack Obama, who later appointed her as
secretary of state.

Amelia Earhart

**First woman to fly solo
across the Atlantic**
1897-1937

Adventure is worthwhile in itself.

In May, 1932, Amelia Earhart flew solo across the Atlantic, struggling through stormy weather. When Earhart landed safely in Ireland she became an immediate international sensation. Her record-smashing string of daring aeronautic feats ended tragically in 1937, when the pioneering aviator attempted to fly around the world, with navigator Fred Noonan. No trace of the plane was ever discovered.

Madame Marie Curie

First woman to win the Nobel Prize
1867-1934

*I am one of those who think like Nobel,
that humanity will draw more good
than evil from new discoveries.*

Maria Sklodowska was born in Warsaw and in 1891 went to Paris to study. There she met and married Pierre Curie. Their research together led to the isolation of polonium and radium. She and her husband were awarded the Nobel Prize for physics in 1903. In 1911 she received another Nobel Prize in chemistry.

Mary Baker Eddy

**First American woman to
found a major religion**
1821-1910

Matter and death are mortal illusions.

Mary Baker Eddy's recovery from ill health
by means of spiritual healing led to her
founding of Christian Science. Overcoming obstacles and a culture unsupportive of
women in public, Eddy employed brilliant
leadership skills and vision to establish a
major religion and national newspaper,
becoming for a time the most powerful
woman in America.

Jane Goodall

Ground-breaking primatologist and environmental activist
1934-

The greatest danger to our future is apathy.

After having assisted anthropologist Louis Leakey, Goodall began her career by living alone in the African forest in order to study chimpanzees. Her observations of chimps' social and tool-making skills blurred the defining line between humans and other primates. A visionary environmental activist, she has written many books and garnered many awards, and founded the Jane Goodall Institute for Wildlife Research, Education and Conservation.

Katharine Graham

First female media mogul
1917-2001

*To love what you do and feel that it matters—
how could anything be more fun?*

Katharine Graham reigned as publisher of
The Washington Post from 1963 to 1993,
becoming one of America's most influential
women. During her tenure she champi-
oned the first amendment by publishing
the controversial Pentagon Papers and by
covering the Watergate scandal, forcing the
resignation of President Richard Nixon. In
1998 she won the Pulitzer Prize for her
best-selling memoir, *Personal History*.

Martha Graham

Pioneer of American modern dance
1894-1991

*Our arms start from the back because
they were once wings.*

Considered one of the great artists of the twentieth century, dancer and choreographer Martha Graham helped establish modern dance as an American art form. Graham performed until the age of 75 and, in 1976, was awarded the Medal of Freedom. Featuring American themes with strong female characters, the Martha Graham Dance Company continues to carry on her legacy.

Nadine Gordimer

**Writer, political activist,
and Nobel Laureate**
1923-

*Truth isn't always beauty,
but the hunger for it is.*

Born in South Africa, where she has
remained all her life, Nadine Gordimer has
always opposed apartheid, both in her writ-
ings and in her political activities. A political novelist with hundreds of short stories
and essays to her credit as well, Gordimer
has also been active in HIV/AIDS causes.
She was awarded the Booker Prize in 1974,
the Nobel Prize for Literature in 1991, and
the Legion of Honor in 2007.

Karen Horney

First feminist psychoanalyst
1885-1952

Like all sciences and all valuations, the psychology of women has hitherto been considered only from the point of view of men.

After arriving in the U.S. from Germany, Karen Horney became assistant director of the Chicago Institute of Psychoanalysis. Forced out of the New York Psychoanalytic Institute for rejecting Freud's view that women were disadvantaged because of their anatomy, she established the Association for the Advancement of Psychoanalysis, the first independent school of psychoanalysis founded by a woman.

Helen Keller

**A powerful symbol of triumph
over adversity**

1880-1968

*One can never consent to creep when one
feels an impulse to soar.*

Blind and deaf from the age of 19 months,
Helen Keller grew into a wild child. But in
1887 her life changed when Anne Sullivan
opened the door to the world of commu-
nication, teaching her to read, write, and
speak. Against all odds, Helen Keller went
on to graduate from Radcliffe in 1904, becoming a champion for the blind and deaf
worldwide—visiting 35 countries, writing
14 books, and meeting 6 U.S. presidents.

Pioneering tennis champion
1943-

*Be bold. If you're going to make
an error, make a doozy, and don't
be afraid to hit the ball.*

For most of the sixties and seventies, King
won nearly every major tennis world championship, a feat few others, male or female,
could claim. She won a record 20 Wim-
bledon titles, including six singles titles. In
1973 she beat tennis champion Bobby
Riggs in a much-publicized "battle of the
sexes." Even more, she has been a pioneer,
fighting for equal rights—and prize
money—for women athletes.

Maya Lin

**Visionary architect of the
Vietnam Veterans Memorial**
1959-

*I try to give people a different way of look-
ing at their surroundings. That's art to me.*

As an architecture student at Yale Univer-
sity, Maya Lin designed the Vietnam Veterans Memorial in Washington, D.C., as part
of a class project. Selected from among
1,421 entries, her bold and unconventional
design brought fierce criticism, but now the
black granite walls inscribed with the names
of 58,000 Americans who died in the
Vietnam War comprise the most-visited
memorial in the nation's capital.

Zora Neale Hurston

**Celebrated African-American
novelist and anthropologist**
1891-1960

*Grab the broom of anger
and drive off the beast of fear.*

Raised in Florida, Zora Neale Hurston
became famous in New York as a literary
catalyst of the Harlem Renaissance. She
graduated from Barnard College and in
1937 wrote *Their Eyes Were Watching God*,
her most famous novel. A Guggenheim
Fellow whose works document African-
American and Haitian folklore, Hurston
was one of the pre-eminent African-
American writers of the twentieth century.

Mary Lyon

**Founder of the first women's
college in the United States**
1797-1849

*Go where no one else will go.
Do what no one else will do.*

In 1837, after three years of traveling and
fundraising, Mary Lyon opened Mount
Holyoke Female Seminary in South
Hadley, Massachusetts. Her aim was to
provide women with the caliber of education available at the finest men's colleges.
The seminary became Mount Holyoke
College. An inspiring model, Mary Lyon
empowered women to intellectual and
non-traditional achievement.

Clare Booth Luce

**First woman ambassador
to a major power**
1903-1987

Because I am a woman, I must make unusual efforts to succeed. If I fail, no one will say, "She doesn't have what it takes." They will say, "Women don't have what it takes."

A prominent Republican, Luce served in Congress and broke barriers as the first female U.S. ambassador, serving in Italy and Brazil. Luce also wrote several plays, including *The Women* and *Kiss the Boys Goodbye*, as well as other books. She was awarded the Presidential Medal of Freedom in 1983.

Madonna

**Best-selling female pop artist
of the twentieth century**
1958-

*I stand for freedom of expression,
doing what you believe in,
and going after your dreams.*

Born in Michigan, Madonna Louise Ciccone came to New York to study dance. She sang with several rock bands before releasing her self-titled album in 1983. Her defiant persona contributed to her rising superstardom. She produced three consecutive #1 albums and several more since 2000. Her net worth is over $400 million, with over 200 million records sold worldwide.

Golda Meir

First female prime minister of Israel
1898–1978

*You'll never find a better sparring
partner than adversity.*

Born in Russia but raised in Wisconsin,
Golda Meir moved to Palestine in 1921. In
1948, when Israel won independence, she
became ambassador to the Soviet Union.
Strong-willed, plainspoken, and fiercely
protective of Israel, Meir was elected to the
Knesset in 1949 and was named the country's foreign minister in 1956. In 1969, at
age 71, Golda Meir became Israel's first
female prime minister.

Wilma Mankiller

**First woman chief of the
Cherokee Nation**

1945-

*A lot of young girls have looked to
their career paths and have said they'd
like to be chief. There's been a change
in the limits people see.*

Wilma Mankiller was the first woman
deputy chief of the Cherokee Nation, serving
as primary chief until 1995. A visionary
and activist leader, she continues to work to
improve the health and education of the
Cherokee people. In 1998, President Clinton
awarded her the Presidential Medal of
Honor, the nation's highest civilian honor.

Sandra Day O'Connor

First woman justice of the Supreme Court

1930-

The power I exert on the court depends on the power of my arguments, not on my gender.

When she could not get a job with a law firm because she was a woman, O'Connor opened her own law firm. Known as tough and conservative, she later became an Arizona state senator and a judge for the Arizona Court of Appeals. In 1981 she became one of America's most influential women as the first female U.S. Supreme Court justice.

Mother Teresa

**Nobel Peace Prize-winning
humanitarian**
1910-1997

*We can do no great things, only
small things with great love.*

Agnes Gonhxa Bojaxhiu decided at age 12
that her future was as a missionary. She left
her native Macedonia to train first in Ireland and then went to India where, in
1950, she started her own order. Through
her tireless work in Calcutta, her mission
grew to more than 400 sisters in 123 countries, establishing orphanages, homes for
lepers, the crippled, those with HIV/AIDS,
and many more.

Rosa Parks

Catalyst for the U. S. civil rights movement
1913-2005

I'm just an average citizen. Many black people before me were arrested for defying the bus laws. They prepared the way.

Born in Tuskegee, Alabama, Rosa Parks opened the door to integration in 1955 in a daring refusal to give up her bus seat to a white man—a right that was upheld by the Supreme Court in a landmark ruling the following year. A civil rights pioneer and activist, Parks received the Presidential Medal of Freedom in 1996.

Frances Perkins

First woman member of the
U.S. Cabinet
1882-1965

*Most of man's problems upon this planet,
in the long history of the race, have been
met and solved either partially or as a
whole by experiment based on common
sense and carried out with courage.*

As secretary of labor under President
Franklin D. Roosevelt for 12 years, Frances
Perkins led the battle against the Great Depression. She helped to reform working
conditions through the passage of legisla-
tion such as the Social Security Act and the
Fair Labor Standards Act.

Georgia O'Keeffe

**One of the greatest artists of
the twentieth century**
1887-1986

*To create one's own world in any
of the arts takes courage.*

Despite her conventional art training,
Georgia O'Keeffe became a unique painter.
Her interest in Oriental art led her away
from the traditional, and a visit to Taos,
New Mexico, led to her residence there and
to a bold and large-scale painting style. Her
lush abstract representations of flowers and
unusual landscapes became the start of a
new American art form.

Sally K. Ride

**First American woman astronaut
to fly in space
1951-**

*I didn't come into the space program
to be the first woman in space. I came
in to get a chance to fly as soon as I could.
The thing that I'll remember about
the flight is that it was fun.*

In 1978, Sally Ride was chosen by
NASA—from a pool of 8,000 applicants—
to become a member of the astronaut pro-
gram. On June 18, 1983, when the shuttle
Challenger lifted off, Ride became the first
American woman to enter outer space.

Eleanor Roosevelt

"First Lady of the world"
1884-1962

*It's better to light a candle than
to curse the darkness.*

Repeatedly voted the most admired woman in international polls, First Lady Eleanor Roosevelt visited almost every war front in World War II. She held press conferences, traveled the country, gave radio addresses, and wrote a weekly newspaper column. Later, as chairman of the UN Commission on Human Rights, she aided the adoption in 1948 of the Universal Declaration of Human Rights.

Gloria Steinem

Feminist and writer
1934-

I have yet to hear a man ask for advice on how to combine marriage and a career.

In 1972 Gloria Steinem founded *Ms.*, a groundbreaking magazine written, edited, and published by women. Author, lecturer, editor, and eloquent political activist, she also played a key role in the National Organization for Women, and helped found the Women's Action Alliance to fight discrimination against women. Her bestselling books include *Outrageous Acts and Everyday Rebellions* and *Revolution from Within: A Book of Self-Esteem*.

Aung San Suu Kyi

Winner of the Nobel Peace Prize
1945-

It is not power that corrupts but fear.

Born in Burma (Myanmar), Aung San Suu Kyi helped found the National League for Democracy in 1988 to resist the brutal military regime. She was influenced by a philosophy of non-violence and Buddhist beliefs. In 1989 she was put under house arrest by Myanmar's government. Dr. Suu Kyi has been in detention, on and off, since that time. In 1990 she won the national election, but the regime ignored the election results. She won the Nobel Peace Prize in 1991.

Wilma Rudolph

First American woman to win three gold medals in one Olympics
1940-1994

No matter what accomplishments you make, somebody helps you.

Wilma Rudolph was a sickly child, and developed polio when she was four years old. Her mother helped her to walk again, and by her senior year in high school she qualified for the 1956 Olympics in track—winning a bronze medal! She went on to take three gold medals in the 1960 Olympics, becoming one of the most famous female athletes of all time.

Margaret Thatcher

Britain's first female prime minister
1925-

*Being powerful is like being a lady. If you
have to tell people you are, you aren't.*

Margaret Thatcher was elected to office
in 1979 and served for three terms, guid-
ing Britain brilliantly through its worst
recession in 50 years. A decisive pragma-
tist who dared to challenge the status
quo, the "iron lady" renewed Britain's
economy and its standing in the global
community. She resigned on November
22, 1990, leaving her indelible impres-
sion on Britain and international politics.

First female TV anchor

1929-

To feel valued, to know, even if only once in a while, that you can do a job well is an absolutely marvelous feeling.

Barbara Walters made history in 1974 when she became the first woman to co-anchor a network evening news show. Years later, she began co-hosting one of television's most popular shows ever—*20/20*. Walters has interviewed high-profile stars and statesmen, including every U. S. president since Nixon. She produces her own specials.

Oprah Winfrey

**Ground-breaking media mogul
and philanthropist**
1954-

*Devote today to something so daring even
you can't believe you're doing it.*

Oprah Winfrey overcame a difficult childhood to become one of the 100 Most Influential People of the 20th Century (*Time* magazine). Since her debut as the first African-American woman to host a national talk show, which earned her multiple Emmy Awards, Oprah has succeeded as well in film, magazines, and books. The world's first black billionaire, Oprah has used her wealth and fame to support causes all over the world.

"Babe" Didrikson Zaharias

First woman of American sports
1914-1956

*I don't seem able to do my best unless
I'm behind or in trouble.*

A versatile athlete, Zaharias won gold medals (and set world's records) in the javelin throw and 80-meter hurdles at the 1932 Olympics. She won 17 straight golf tournaments in 1946-47, becoming the first American winner of the British Women's Amateur championship. In 1999, *Sports Illustrated* named her Individual Female Athlete of the Century.

Harriet Tubman

The "Moses" of her people
1820-1913

Always remember, you have within you the strength, the patience, and the passion to reach for the stars to change the world.

Harriet Tubman was a runaway slave who served as a "conductor" on the Underground Railroad. Brave and committed, she not only helped free more than 800 slaves, but during the Civil War she also worked for the Union as a spy, scout, and nurse. After the war, Tubman's civil rights activism shifted to women's suffrage and working to fund schools for former slaves.

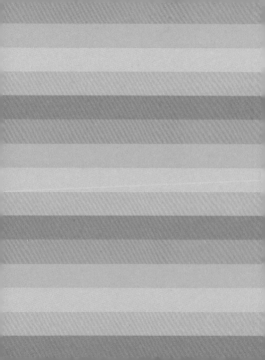